10.2015

W9-AGB-183

Snowboarding GREATS

BY LORI POLYDOROS

Reading Consultant:
Barbara J. Fox
Professor Emerita
North Carolina State University

CAPSTONE PRESS
a capstone imprint

Blazers is published by Capstone Press,
1710 Roe Crest Drive, North Mankato, Minnesota, 56003
www.capstonepub.com

Library of Congress Cataloging-in-Publication Data
Polydoros, Lori, 1969–
　　Snowboarding greats / by Lori Polydoros.
　　p. cm. — (Blazers. Best of the best.)
　　Includes bibliographical references and index.
　　Summary: "Lists and describes the best competitive snowboarders in the world"—Provided
by publisher.
ISBN 978-1-4296-8434-7 (library binding)
ISBN 978-1-62065-206-0 (ebook PDF)
1. Snowboarders—Juvenile literature. I. Title.
GV857.S57P67 2013
796.9390922—dc23[B]   2012000119

Editorial Credits
Mandy Robbins, editor; Kyle Grenz, designer; Laura Manthe, production specialist

Photo Credits
Corbis: Bo Bridges, 12-13, Icon SMI/Marc Piscotty, 14-15; Dreamstime: Kaleb Timberlake, back
cover; Getty Images: AFP/Morten Holm, 22-23, Ben Liebenberg, 28-29, Brian Bahr, 26-27, Doug
Pensinger, 10-11, 18-19, WireImage/Nathan Shanahan, 21; Newscom: AFLO Sports/Christopher
Jue, 8-9, EPA/Andrew Gombert, 1 (bottom), cover (bottom), EPA/Arno Balzarini, cover (top),
EPA/Jean-Christophe Bott, 1 (top), Getty Images/AFP/Adrian Dennis, 4-5, Getty Images/AFP/
Javier Soriano, 6-7, Icon SMI/DPPI/Vincent Curutchet, 24; Russell Dalby, www.russelldalby.com,
16-17

Artistic Effects
iStockphoto: Ian Harding, (background)

**The publisher highly recommends that anyone attempting to ride a snowboard or perform
snowboarding tricks should wear the appropriate safety gear.**

**The publisher does not endorse products whose logos may appear on objects in images in
this book.**

Printed in the United States of America in Stevens Point, Wisconsin.
032012   006678WZF12

TABLE OF CONTENTS

Bigger, Faster, Stronger

Snowboarders race down steep slopes and flip off snowy ramps. Most pros learn to snowboard as children. With talent and hard work, they ride to the top!

Lindsey Jacobellis
(1985-)

Lindsey Jacobellis entered her first Winter X Games at age 15. Since then she has won seven gold medals. Lindsey competes in **snowboardcross** (SBX), **slopestyle**, and **half-pipe** events.

snowboardcross—a mix between alpine and freestyle in which snowboarders race around obstacles

slopestyle—a freestyle performance of tricks and jumps combined with an obstacle course

half-pipe—a U-shaped ramp with high walls; snowboarders soar off half-pipes to do tricks in midair

Stevie Bell
(1985-)

Stevie Bell pulls off amazing tricks. In 2006 he became a member of the Forum Pro Team. Stevie shows off his wild moves in many snowboarding movies.

FACT Only the best snowboarders are asked to be part of the Forum Pro Team. Stevie starred in the team's video *That* in 2006.

Danny Kass
(1982-)

Danny Kass is amazing in the **superpipe**. He won five U.S. Open Superpipe Championships. Danny also won seven Winter X Games medals and two Winter Olympic silver medals.

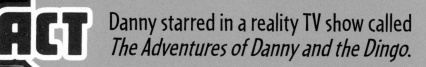

FACT Danny starred in a reality TV show called *The Adventures of Danny and the Dingo.*

superpipe–a half-pipe with walls higher than a normal half-pipe; superpipes are often used at professional competitions

Andreas Wiig
(1981-)

Andreas Wiig's style and ability to spin make him a tough competitor. Andreas won back-to-back gold medals in the Winter X Games in 2007 and 2008.

Kevin Pearce
(1981-)

In 2008 Kevin Pearce competed in three Winter X Games events in one day. He earned two medals that day. Kevin suffered a brain injury while training for the 2010 Winter Olympics. He is recovering and hopes to compete in snowboarding again.

TRICKED OUT!

LOOP
a complete flip on a snowboard,
either forward or backward

Gigi Rüf
(1981–)

Gigi Rüf is famous for tricks such as the loop. In 2009 *Snowboarder Magazine* named him one of their riders of the year. Gigi has starred in more snowboarding videos than almost any other rider.

Shaun Palmer

(1968–)

Shaun Palmer leads the way in SBX. He won three gold medals and two silvers in SBX at the Winter X Games. The newspaper *USA Today* has called Shaun "the world's greatest athlete."

FACT Shaun also competes in motocross, skiing, mountain biking, and car racing.

Nicolas Muller
(1982-)

Nicolas Muller enjoys pulling off tricks out in the wilderness. He has starred in many snowboarding videos. Nicolas was named one of *Snowboarder Magazine*'s riders of the year in 2006 and 2008.

FACT Nicolas is very involved in protecting the **environment**.

environment–the natural world
of the land, water, and air

Terje Haakonsen
(1974-)

Terje Haakonsen won the Burton European Open Snowboarding Championship in half-pipe five times. He also won the Mt. Baker Legendary Banked Slalom six times. The Haakon flip is a trick named after Terje.

TRICKED OUT!

HAAKON FLIP
the rider launches off a half-pipe backward and performs a 720-degree rotation

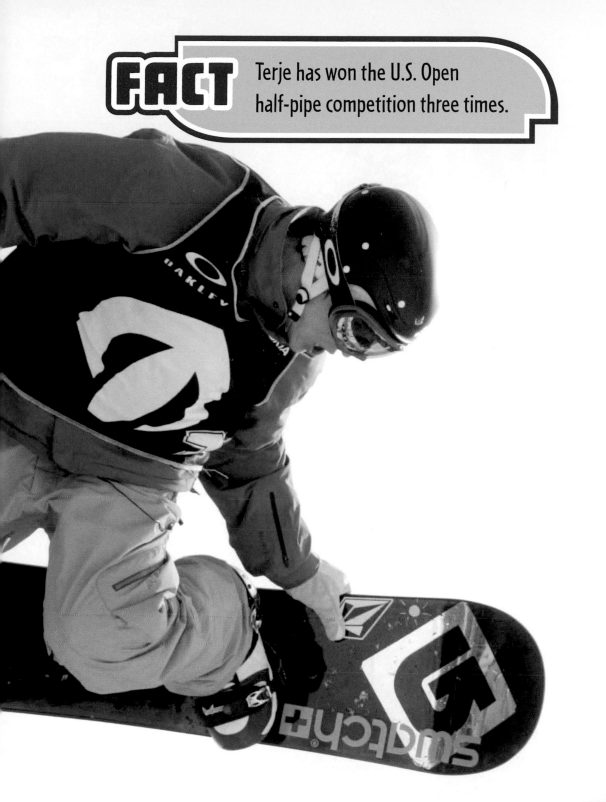

FACT Terje has won the U.S. Open half-pipe competition three times.

Shaun White
(1986-)

Shaun White is known for his creative trick **combinations**. He has won medals in every Winter X Games he has competed in. More than 10 of these medals are gold.

combination–a mixture of two or more tricks strung together

Travis Rice
(1982-)

Travis Rice is a Winter X Games gold medalist. He competes in backcountry, **park**, and half-pipe events. Travis has also starred in several snowboarding movies.

park–an event with freestyle snowboarding in snowboard parks that can include jumps, rails, and ramps

John Jackson

(1983-)

Like Travis Rice, John Jackson stars in snowboarding movies. In 2010 he won *Snowboarder Magazine*'s rider, jumper, and video of the year awards. John's double cork trick has taken snowboarding to the next level.

TRICKED OUT!

DOUBLE CORK
when a rider spins parallel to the ground through two full rotations

GLOSSARY

combination (KAHM-buh-nay-shun)—a mixture of two or more tricks strung together

environment (in-VY-ruhn-muhnt)—the natural world of the land, water, and air

half-pipe (HAF-pipe)—a U-shaped ramp with high walls

park (PARK)—an event with freestyle snowboarding in snowboard parks that can include jumps, rails, and ramps

slopestyle (SLOHP-stile)—a freestyle performance of tricks and jumps combined with an obstacle course

snowboardcross (SNOH-bord-krawss)—a mix between alpine and freestyle in which snowboarders race around obstacles

superpipe (SOO-pur-pipe)—a halfpipe with walls higher than a normal halfpipe; superpipes are often used at professional competitions

READ MORE

Gitlin, Marty. *Shaun White: Snow and Skateboard Champion.* Hot Celebrity Biographies. Berkeley Heights, N.J.: Enslow Publishers, Inc., 2009.

Miller, Connie Colwell. *Snowboarding Slopestyle.* X Games. Mankato, Minn.: Capstone Press, 2008.

INTERNET SITES

FactHound offers a safe, fun way to find Internet sites related to this book. All of the sites on FactHound have been researched by our staff.

Here's all you do:

Visit *www.facthound.com*

Type in this code: 9781429684347

Check out projects, games and lots more at
www.capstonekids.com

INDEX